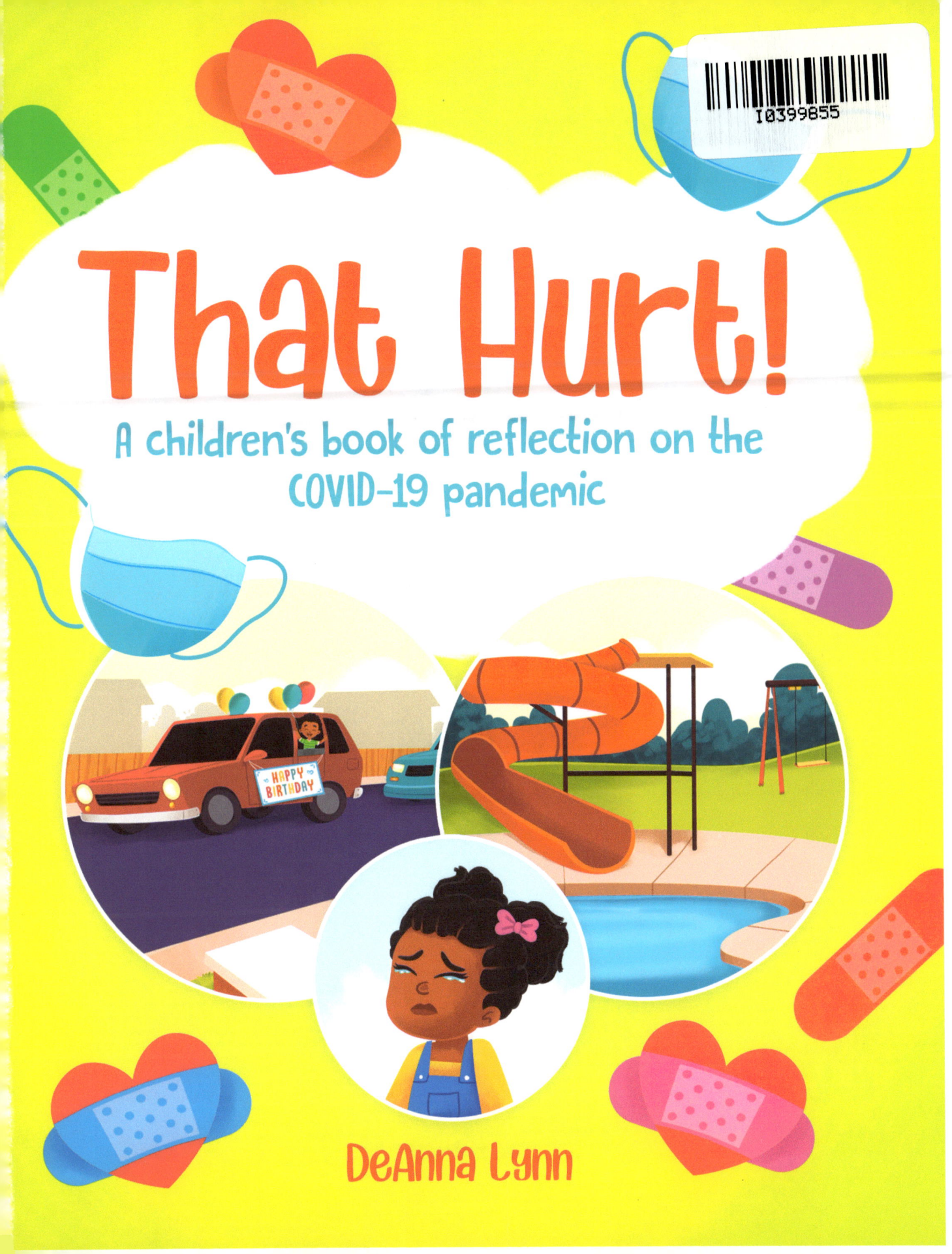

Written by: DeAnna Lynn
Illustrated by: Arnab Chakraborty

Copyright 2021 by DeAnna Lynn

Published by SOAR Press

All rights reserved.
No part of this publication may be reproduced, stored in a retrieval system, or transmitted in any form or by any means, electronic, mechanical, photocopying, recording, or otherwise, without written permission of the publisher.

To essential workers worldwide:
we owe it all to you. Thank you.

Before the zooms, before the "get wells," before the wipes flew off the shelves...

After nachos, after spills, after arenas packed to the gills...

Behind all the emails,
behind new routines,
behind the muted video screens...

In bags, in carts, delivering with a hopeful heart...

After cheese was sprinkled, after sundaes were topped, after all the popcorn kernels popped...

...with t-shirts to be tossed,
we wore them safely.

...between nature movies to discover, we watched our favorites.

Across the yard, across the street, across empty tables where we'd eat...

...across the miles, parties felt incomplete,
but we were still there.

As swings swung empty, as beaches closed,
as waterparks and pools saw few of us go...

Through noisy homes, through winter weather, through the fights that made us better...

...though staying at home felt like forever, we faced the changes.

...by having long hugs with our families, we named our feelings.

Hearing the ticks and tocks, giving waves from the mailbox...

...seeing the empty street blocks, we kept others safe.

Despite long lines for the test,
despite the coughs that hurt our chests...

...despite trading fun times for rest, we got well.

Having long beards, having silver hair, having cool shirts and pajamas to wear...

...having bigger and stronger muscles to bear,
we looked a little different.

For the marchers, for the speakers, for the heartbroken leaders...

...for the helpers who loved deeper, we admired you.

To the scientists and doctors who taught, to the glimmer of hope they brought...

| Sister | Grandma | Mom |

| Dr. | Friend | Daddy |

...to the angels always in our thoughts, we salute you.

www.ingramcontent.com/pod-product-compliance
Lightning Source LLC
Chambersburg PA
CBHW040021130526
44590CB00036B/53